EMMANUEL JOSEPH

Eco-Coins and Empires The Billionaires Merging Crypto, Sustainability, and Global Power

Copyright © 2025 by Emmanuel Joseph

All rights reserved. No part of this publication may be reproduced, stored or transmitted in any form or by any means, electronic, mechanical, photocopying, recording, scanning, or otherwise without written permission from the publisher. It is illegal to copy this book, post it to a website, or distribute it by any other means without permission.

First edition

This book was professionally typeset on Reedsy.
Find out more at reedsy.com

Contents

1	Chapter 1: The Dawn of a New Era	1
2	Chapter 2: The Green Blockchain	3
3	Chapter 3: Pioneers of the Eco-Coin Movement	5
4	Chapter 4: Environmental Impact and Innovations	7
5	Chapter 5: The Global Ecosystem	9
6	Chapter 6: Technological Challenges and Solutions	11
7	Chapter 7: The Role of Education and Awareness	13
8	Chapter 8: Case Studies of Success	15
9	Chapter 9: The Intersection of Technology and Policy	17
10	Chapter 10: The Future of Eco-Coins	19
11	Chapter 11: The Rise of Digital Empires	21
12	Chapter 12: Challenges and Controversies	23
13	Chapter 13: The Power of Collaboration	25
14	Chapter 14: The Impact on Global Power Dynamics	27
15	Chapter 15: The Role of Innovation in Driving Change	29
16	Chapter 16: Lessons Learned and Future Directions	31
17	Chapter 17: A Vision for the Future	33

1

Chapter 1: The Dawn of a New Era

In the early 21st century, as environmental crises loomed and technological revolutions accelerated, a new breed of visionary billionaires emerged. These titans of industry saw beyond the immediate profit and recognized the profound opportunities within the marriage of cryptocurrency and sustainability. They envisioned a world where digital finance could drive environmental change, breaking away from the traditional paradigms that had long governed both sectors. It was a bold and unprecedented leap, filled with both promise and peril.

These innovators were not merely looking to make a quick fortune. Instead, they were driven by a deep-seated belief in the transformative power of technology. They understood that the blockchain, the backbone of cryptocurrencies, could offer unparalleled transparency and efficiency, qualities sorely needed in the fight against climate change. They also recognized the potential for these digital assets to democratize access to financial systems, providing an inclusive platform for global economic participation. In essence, they were crafting a new narrative, one that intertwined the fate of the planet with the future of finance.

Central to their vision was the concept of Eco-Coins, digital currencies designed with sustainability at their core. Unlike traditional cryptocurrencies, Eco-Coins were engineered to incentivize environmentally friendly practices. Whether through rewarding carbon offsetting initiatives or funding renewable energy projects, these coins were positioned as catalysts for ecological innovation. The underlying technology ensured that every transaction contributed to a greener future, creating a self-sustaining ecosystem that aligned financial gain with environmental stewardship.

The journey was fraught with challenges. Skepticism abounded, both from traditional financial institutions and environmental advocates wary of the crypto world. Yet, the commitment of these billionaires to their cause was unwavering. They invested not just their wealth but their influence, leveraging their positions to foster collaboration across industries and governments. It was a testament to their belief in a better future, one where economic powerhouses could be the architects of sustainable development.

2

Chapter 2: The Green Blockchain

The cornerstone of the Eco-Coin revolution was the green blockchain, a technological marvel that redefined the principles of digital finance. Unlike its predecessors, which were often criticized for their energy-intensive processes, the green blockchain was designed with sustainability at its heart. This innovative ledger system utilized renewable energy sources and advanced algorithms to minimize its carbon footprint, making it a paragon of eco-friendly technology.

The green blockchain operated on a decentralized network, ensuring that power and control were distributed across a vast array of nodes. This decentralization not only enhanced security but also fostered a sense of community and collective responsibility. Each participant in the network played a role in maintaining its integrity, creating a robust and resilient system that could withstand external pressures. Moreover, the transparency inherent in blockchain technology ensured that every transaction was verifiable and traceable, eliminating the possibility of fraud and corruption.

The integration of smart contracts was another revolutionary aspect of the green blockchain. These self-executing contracts automatically enforced the terms of an agreement, reducing the need for intermediaries and streamlining processes. In the context of Eco-Coins, smart contracts facilitated the direct allocation of funds to environmental projects, ensuring that resources were utilized efficiently and effectively. This innovation empowered individuals and organizations to engage in sustainable practices with ease, knowing that their efforts were being rewarded transparently and promptly.

The development of the green blockchain was a collaborative effort, bringing together some of the brightest minds in technology, finance, and environmental science. It was a testament to what could be achieved when diverse disciplines united towards a common goal. This interdisciplinary approach not only accelerated technological advancements but also fostered a culture of innovation and creativity. As the green blockchain continued to evolve, it became the bedrock upon which the future of sustainable finance was built.

3

Chapter 3: Pioneers of the Eco-Coin Movement

The rise of Eco-Coins would not have been possible without the vision and determination of pioneering billionaires who championed the cause. Among them was Emilia Clarke, a former tech entrepreneur who transitioned into the world of sustainable finance. Clarke's journey began when she recognized the potential for blockchain technology to revolutionize environmental conservation. She founded EcoGuard, a company that developed Eco-Coins and spearheaded various green initiatives, quickly becoming a leader in the movement.

Another key figure was Raj Patel, a philanthropist and investor with a passion for renewable energy. Patel's foundation funded numerous research projects aimed at enhancing the efficiency of solar and wind technologies. He saw Eco-Coins as a means to further incentivize the adoption of clean energy, integrating his investments with the digital currency ecosystem. Patel's influence extended beyond financial contributions; he was a vocal advocate for policy changes that supported the intersection of technology and sustainability.

Isabella Martinez, a former environmental activist turned crypto enthusiast, played a crucial role in raising awareness about Eco-Coins. Martinez's extensive network of grassroots organizations provided a platform for educating the public about the benefits of this new digital currency. She organized conferences and workshops, bringing together experts and enthusiasts to discuss the future of sustainable finance. Martinez's efforts were instrumental in garnering widespread support and fostering a sense of community within the Eco-Coin movement.

These pioneers, along with countless others, formed the backbone of the Eco-Coin revolution. Their combined efforts and unwavering commitment to sustainability drove the movement forward, overcoming obstacles and skepticism. They demonstrated that the convergence of cryptocurrency and environmentalism was not only possible but also essential for addressing the global challenges of the 21st century. Through their leadership and innovation, they paved the way for a new era of eco-conscious finance.

4

Chapter 4: Environmental Impact and Innovations

As Eco-Coins gained traction, their environmental impact became increasingly evident. One of the most significant innovations was the development of carbon offset programs funded by Eco-Coins. These programs incentivized individuals and businesses to reduce their carbon emissions by rewarding them with digital currency. The funds generated were then used to support reforestation projects, renewable energy initiatives, and other green endeavors. This closed-loop system ensured that every transaction contributed to a sustainable future.

Another groundbreaking innovation was the creation of decentralized autonomous organizations (DAOs) focused on environmental conservation. These DAOs operated on the green blockchain, allowing stakeholders to participate in decision-making processes directly. By utilizing smart contracts, DAOs ensured that funds were allocated transparently and efficiently to various eco-friendly projects. This democratic approach empowered communities to take charge of their environmental efforts, fostering a sense of ownership and responsibility.

Eco-Coins also facilitated the development of sustainable supply chains. Blockchain technology enabled the tracking of products from their origin to the end consumer, ensuring that they were sourced and produced ethically.

This transparency allowed consumers to make informed choices, supporting businesses that prioritized sustainability. Additionally, Eco-Coins provided a means of rewarding companies that adhered to eco-friendly practices, further incentivizing the adoption of sustainable supply chains.

The ripple effects of these innovations extended beyond environmental benefits. The increased adoption of Eco-Coins spurred economic growth in underserved communities, providing new opportunities for financial inclusion. By democratizing access to digital finance, Eco-Coins empowered individuals to participate in the global economy, fostering a more equitable and sustainable future. The success of these initiatives demonstrated the transformative potential of merging cryptocurrency with environmentalism, inspiring further advancements and collaborations.

5

Chapter 5: The Global Ecosystem

The adoption of Eco-Coins was not limited to a single region or country; it became a global phenomenon. As nations grappled with the challenges of climate change and economic inequality, many saw the potential of Eco-Coins to address these issues simultaneously. Governments and policymakers began to explore ways to integrate this new digital currency into their existing financial systems, recognizing its potential to drive sustainable development.

One of the first countries to embrace Eco-Coins was Sweden, known for its progressive environmental policies. The Swedish government collaborated with EcoCoin pioneers to develop a national strategy for integrating digital currency into their green economy. This included the implementation of blockchain-based carbon trading systems and the use of Eco-Coins to incentivize renewable energy projects. Sweden's success served as a model for other nations, demonstrating the feasibility and benefits of adopting eco-friendly digital finance.

In Africa, the adoption of Eco-Coins played a crucial role in addressing the continent's unique challenges. Many African countries faced significant barriers to financial inclusion and environmental sustainability. Eco-Coins provided a means of overcoming these obstacles by offering a secure and accessible platform for digital transactions. Initiatives such as microloans for small-scale farmers and funding for clean energy projects helped to improve livelihoods while promoting environmental conservation. The success of these programs highlighted the potential of Eco-Coins to drive positive change in diverse contexts.

The global nature of the Eco-Coin movement also fostered international collaboration. Organizations such as the United Nations and the World Economic Forum recognized the potential of this innovative approach to address global challenges. They facilitated partnerships between governments, businesses, and non-profits, creating a network of stakeholders committed to advancing sustainable finance. This collaborative effort ensured that the benefits of Eco-Coins were distributed equitably, fostering a sense of shared responsibility and collective action.

6

Chapter 6: Technological Challenges and Solutions

The development and implementation of Eco-Coins were not without challenges. One of the most significant hurdles was the scalability of the green blockchain. As the popularity of Eco-Coins grew, so did the demand for processing power and energy. Ensuring that the blockchain remained efficient and sustainable required continuous innovation and adaptation. Researchers and developers worked tirelessly to enhance the algorithms and infrastructure, incorporating advances in renewable energy and energy-efficient computing.

Another challenge was ensuring the security and integrity of the Eco-Coin network. Cybersecurity threats were a constant concern, with potential vulnerabilities posing risks to the entire ecosystem. To address this, developers implemented advanced cryptographic techniques and decentralized architectures to safeguard the network. Regular audits and updates were conducted to identify and mitigate potential threats, ensuring that the system remained robust and resilient.

Regulatory compliance was another critical aspect of the Eco-Coin movement. Navigating the complex landscape of international finance and environmental regulations was no easy feat. The pioneers of the Eco-Coin movement worked closely with policymakers and legal experts to ensure that their innovations complied with existing laws. They also advocated for the development of new regulations that supported the integration of digital finance and sustainability. This collaborative approach not only facilitated the growth of the Eco-Coin ecosystem but also helped to establish standards and best practices for the industry.

Despite these challenges, the determination and ingenuity of the Eco-Coin pioneers prevailed. They continually pushed the boundaries of technology, finding creative solutions to the obstacles they faced. Their efforts demonstrated that it was possible to create a sustainable and secure digital currency that could drive meaningful change. As the Eco-Coin movement continued to evolve, it became a symbol of innovation and resilience in the face of adversity.

7

Chapter 7: The Role of Education and Awareness

Education and awareness played a crucial role in the success of the Eco-Coin movement. From the outset, pioneers recognized the importance of informing the public about the benefits and potential of this new digital currency. They launched comprehensive educational campaigns to demystify blockchain technology and its environmental applications, making it accessible to a wide audience.

Workshops, webinars, and community events were organized to engage people from all walks of life. These initiatives provided a platform for experts to share their knowledge and for participants to ask questions and voice their concerns. By fostering a culture of transparency and open dialogue, the Eco-Coin movement built trust and credibility within the community. This grassroots approach ensured that people felt empowered and informed, enabling them to make educated decisions about their involvement in the movement.

In addition to public education, efforts were made to integrate Eco-Coin concepts into formal education systems. Universities and research institutions partnered with Eco-Coin pioneers to develop curricula and conduct studies on sustainable finance. These academic collaborations helped to legitimize the movement and provided valuable insights into its long-term potential. As a result, a new generation of scholars and professionals emerged, equipped with the knowledge and skills to advance the Eco-Coin revolution.

The media also played a significant role in raising awareness about Eco-Coins. Journalists and influencers highlighted the innovative aspects of this digital currency and its environmental impact, bringing the movement into the mainstream. Through articles, interviews, and social media campaigns, the story of Eco-Coins reached a global audience. This widespread coverage helped to attract new supporters and investors, further driving the growth and success of the movement.

8

Chapter 8: Case Studies of Success

As the Eco-Coin movement gained momentum, numerous success stories emerged, showcasing the transformative potential of this innovative approach. One such case was the partnership between EcoGuard and the government of Costa Rica. Known for its commitment to environmental conservation, Costa Rica saw the potential of Eco-Coins to enhance its sustainability efforts. Through this collaboration, the country implemented blockchain-based carbon offset programs and incentivized renewable energy projects, resulting in significant reductions in carbon emissions.

Another notable success story was the use of Eco-Coins in India to promote sustainable agriculture. Small-scale farmers, often excluded from traditional financial systems, found new opportunities through microloans funded by Eco-Coins. These loans enabled farmers to invest in eco-friendly practices, such as organic farming and water conservation techniques. The increased productivity and environmental benefits generated by these initiatives highlighted the potential of Eco-Coins to drive positive change in diverse contexts.

In Kenya, Eco-Coins played a crucial role in addressing the challenges of financial inclusion and renewable energy access. The adoption of digital currency provided a secure and accessible platform for transactions, empowering individuals and businesses to participate in the global economy.

Additionally, Eco-Coins funded solar energy projects, bringing electricity to remote communities and improving the quality of life for thousands of people. This success demonstrated the potential of Eco-Coins to foster economic growth while promoting sustainability.

These case studies, along with many others, highlighted the transformative impact of the Eco-Coin movement. They showcased the potential of digital currency to address global challenges and drive meaningful change. The success of these initiatives inspired further advancements and collaborations, propelling the movement towards a more sustainable and inclusive future.

9

Chapter 9: The Intersection of Technology and Policy

The success of the Eco-Coin movement was closely tied to the intersection of technology and policy. Recognizing the potential of digital currency to drive sustainable development, policymakers began to explore ways to integrate Eco-Coins into existing regulatory frameworks. This collaborative approach ensured that the benefits of Eco-Coins were maximized while minimizing potential risks.

One of the key policy innovations was the development of blockchain-based carbon trading systems. These systems allowed countries to trade carbon credits transparently and efficiently, incentivizing emissions reductions and supporting global climate goals. By integrating Eco-Coins into these systems, policymakers ensured that the financial gains from carbon trading were reinvested into sustainable projects. This closed-loop approach created a self-sustaining ecosystem that aligned economic incentives with environmental stewardship.

Another significant policy development was the establishment of international standards for sustainable finance. Organizations such as the United Nations and the World Economic Forum played a crucial role in facilitating dialogue and collaboration between governments, businesses, and non-profits. These efforts resulted in the creation of guidelines and best practices for the integration of digital currency and sustainability. By providing a clear framework for action, these standards helped to foster trust and credibility within the Eco-Coin movement.

The collaboration between technology and policy also extended to the development of public-private partnerships. Governments and private sector leaders recognized the potential of Eco-Coins to address global challenges and drive innovation. By pooling resources and expertise, these partnerships accelerated the growth of the Eco-Coin ecosystem and facilitated the implementation of sustainable initiatives. This collaborative approach ensured that the benefits of Eco-Coins were distributed equitably, fostering a sense of shared responsibility and collective action.

10

Chapter 10: The Future of Eco-Coins

As the Eco-Coin movement continued to evolve, its future prospects remained bright. The advancements in blockchain technology and the growing commitment to sustainability provided a solid foundation for further growth and innovation. The pioneers of the Eco-Coin movement remained dedicated to their vision, continually pushing the boundaries of what was possible.

One of the most promising areas of development was the integration of artificial intelligence (AI) and machine learning into the Eco-Coin ecosystem. These technologies offered new opportunities for enhancing the efficiency and effectiveness of sustainable finance. AI algorithms could analyze vast amounts of data to identify trends and opportunities, enabling more informed decision-making. Machine learning could optimize smart contracts, ensuring that resources were allocated efficiently and effectively. The combination of AI and Eco-Coins promised to drive significant advancements in the field of sustainable finance.

The global adoption of Eco-Coins also held promise for addressing some of the most pressing challenges of the 21st century. As nations continued to grapple with climate change, economic inequality, and financial exclusion, Eco-Coins offered a powerful tool for driving positive change. By aligning economic incentives with environmental stewardship, Eco-Coins provided a means of fostering sustainable development on a global scale. The continued success of the movement depended on the collective efforts of governments, businesses, and individuals, working together towards a common goal.

The future of Eco-Coins was not without its challenges. The pioneers of the movement recognized the need for continuous innovation and adaptation to address emerging risks and opportunities. They remained committed to their vision, dedicated to creating a more sustainable and inclusive future. As the Eco-Coin movement continued to evolve, it became a symbol of hope and resilience in the face of global challenges.

11

Chapter 11: The Rise of Digital Empires

The impact of Eco-Coins extended beyond environmental benefits; it also reshaped the global economic landscape. The pioneers of the movement, through their vision and determination, built digital empires that spanned continents and industries. These empires were characterized by their commitment to sustainability and innovation, driving positive change on a global scale.

One of the most prominent digital empires was EcoGuard, founded by Emilia Clarke. EcoGuard's success was built on its innovative approach to sustainable finance and its commitment to transparency and inclusivity. Through strategic partnerships and investments, EcoGuard expanded its influence across various sectors, from renewable energy to sustainable agriculture. The company's achievements demonstrated the potential of Eco-Coins to drive economic growth while promoting environmental stewardship.

Raj Patel's foundation also emerged as a powerful digital empire, leveraging its resources and expertise to advance the Eco-Coin movement. Patel's investments in renewable energy and sustainable projects created a positive feedback loop, generating both financial returns and environmental benefits. The foundation's impact extended beyond financial contributions; it also played a crucial role in shaping policy and fostering international collaboration. Patel's vision of a more sustainable and inclusive world became a reality through the success of his digital empire.

The rise of digital empires also highlighted the potential of Eco-Coins to drive social change. Isabella Martinez's grassroots organizations, supported by Eco-Coins, empowered communities to take charge of their environmental efforts. These organizations provided a platform for education, advocacy, and collaboration, fostering a sense of ownership and responsibility. The success of these initiatives demonstrated that the power of Eco-Coins extended beyond financial transactions, driving meaningful change at the community level.

12

Chapter 12: Challenges and Controversies

The rapid growth of the Eco-Coin movement was not without its challenges and controversies. Critics raised concerns about the potential risks and unintended consequences of this new digital currency. Some argued that the rapid expansion of Eco-Coins could lead to market instability and financial speculation. Others questioned the long-term sustainability of blockchain technology, citing concerns about energy consumption and scalability.

To address these concerns, the pioneers of the Eco-Coin movement emphasized the importance of continuous innovation and adaptation. They invested in research and development to enhance the efficiency and sustainability of the green blockchain. Efforts were also made to promote responsible investing and to educate the public about the potential risks and benefits of Eco-Coins. By fostering a culture of transparency and accountability, the movement sought to build trust and credibility within the community.

Another controversy was the potential for regulatory challenges and conflicts with existing financial systems. As the adoption of Eco-Coins grew, policymakers grappled with the complexities of integrating digital currency into traditional financial systems. The pioneers of the Eco-Coin movement recognized the importance of collaboration and dialogue with regulators to address these challenges. They advocated for the development of clear and consistent regulations that supported the integration of digital currency and sustainability. This collaborative approach helped to mitigate potential conflicts and ensure the long-term success of the Eco-Coin movement.

Despite these controversies, the pioneers of the Eco-Coin movement remained committed to their vision. They recognized that the challenges and criticisms were part of the growing pains of an innovative and disruptive movement. By addressing these issues head-on and fostering a culture of transparency and accountability, they demonstrated the resilience and adaptability necessary for long-term success. The Eco-Coin movement continued to evolve and thrive, driven by the unwavering determination of its pioneers.

13

Chapter 13: The Power of Collaboration

C ollaboration was a cornerstone of the Eco-Coin movement, driving its success and impact on a global scale. The pioneers recognized that addressing the complex challenges of the 21st century required a collective effort, bringing together diverse stakeholders from various sectors and regions. This collaborative approach fostered innovation, knowledge-sharing, and the pooling of resources, creating a robust and resilient ecosystem.

One of the key collaborations was between the Eco-Coin pioneers and international organizations such as the United Nations and the World Economic Forum. These partnerships facilitated dialogue and coordination on global initiatives, aligning efforts towards common goals. The collaboration with the United Nations, for example, led to the development of blockchain-based solutions for tracking and achieving the Sustainable Development Goals (SDGs). By integrating Eco-Coins into these initiatives, the movement ensured that financial incentives were aligned with global sustainability objectives.

Another significant collaboration was between the Eco-Coin pioneers and the private sector. Companies from various industries, including technology, finance, and energy, recognized the potential of Eco-Coins to drive innovation and sustainability. These partnerships resulted in the development of new products and services that leveraged the benefits of digital currency and blockchain technology. For example, tech companies developed applications that facilitated the use of Eco-Coins for everyday transactions, while energy companies integrated blockchain-based solutions for tracking and trading renewable energy credits.

The collaboration between the Eco-Coin movement and grassroots organizations was also crucial for its success. These organizations provided a platform for engaging communities and raising awareness about the benefits of Eco-Coins. They played a vital role in educating the public, advocating for policy changes, and fostering a sense of ownership and responsibility. By working together, the Eco-Coin pioneers and grassroots organizations created a powerful and inclusive movement that resonated with people from all walks of life.

14

Chapter 14: The Impact on Global Power Dynamics

The rise of Eco-Coins and the digital empires they spawned had a profound impact on global power dynamics. Traditional power structures, long dominated by established financial institutions and nation-states, were disrupted by the emergence of decentralized and inclusive digital finance. The pioneers of the Eco-Coin movement, through their vision and innovation, challenged the status quo and reshaped the global economic landscape.

One of the most significant shifts was the democratization of access to financial systems. Eco-Coins provided a secure and accessible platform for digital transactions, empowering individuals and communities that had been excluded from traditional financial systems. This democratization fostered economic growth and inclusion, particularly in underserved regions. The success of these initiatives demonstrated the potential of digital currency to drive positive change and promote social equity.

The rise of digital empires also challenged the dominance of traditional financial institutions. Companies like EcoGuard and Raj Patel's foundation leveraged their resources and expertise to drive innovation and sustainability, creating new centers of power and influence. These digital empires operated with a commitment to transparency, inclusivity, and environmental stewardship, setting a new standard for corporate responsibility. Their success inspired other companies to adopt similar principles, further driving the shift towards a more sustainable and equitable global economy.

The impact of Eco-Coins on global power dynamics also extended to the realm of international relations. As nations recognized the potential of digital currency to drive sustainable development, they began to explore ways to integrate Eco-Coins into their economic strategies. This resulted in new alliances and partnerships, as countries collaborated on blockchain-based solutions for addressing global challenges. The success of these initiatives demonstrated the potential of Eco-Coins to foster international cooperation and drive collective action towards a sustainable future.

15

Chapter 15: The Role of Innovation in Driving Change

Innovation was at the heart of the Eco-Coin movement, driving its success and impact on a global scale. The pioneers of the movement recognized the potential of cutting-edge technologies to address the complex challenges of the 21st century. Through their vision and determination, they continually pushed the boundaries of what was possible, creating new solutions and opportunities for sustainable development.

One of the key innovations was the development of the green blockchain, a technological marvel that redefined the principles of digital finance. This eco-friendly ledger system utilized renewable energy sources and advanced algorithms to minimize its carbon footprint, making it a paragon of sustainability. The green blockchain facilitated the creation of Eco-Coins, digital currencies designed with environmental incentives at their core. This innovative approach ensured that every transaction contributed to a greener future, creating a self-sustaining ecosystem that aligned financial gain with environmental stewardship.

The integration of artificial intelligence (AI) and machine learning into the Eco-Coin ecosystem was another groundbreaking innovation. These technologies offered new opportunities for enhancing the efficiency and effectiveness of sustainable finance. AI algorithms could analyze vast amounts of data to identify trends and opportunities, enabling more informed decision-making. Machine learning could optimize smart contracts, ensuring that resources were allocated efficiently and effectively. The combination of AI and Eco-Coins promised to drive significant advancements in the field of sustainable finance.

The pioneers of the Eco-Coin movement also embraced innovation in their approach to collaboration and partnership. By bringing together diverse stakeholders from various sectors and regions, they created a robust and resilient ecosystem. This collaborative approach fostered knowledge-sharing, resource-pooling, and the development of new products and services. The success of these initiatives demonstrated the power of innovation to drive positive change and create a more sustainable and inclusive future.

16

Chapter 16: Lessons Learned and Future Directions

The Eco-Coin movement provided valuable lessons for the future of sustainable finance. The pioneers of the movement recognized the importance of continuous innovation, adaptation, and collaboration in addressing the complex challenges of the 21st century. Their experiences highlighted the potential of digital currency and blockchain technology to drive meaningful change, while also underscoring the need for responsible and transparent practices.

One of the key lessons learned was the importance of education and awareness in fostering a culture of sustainability. The success of the Eco-Coin movement was closely tied to its efforts to inform and engage the public. Comprehensive educational campaigns, community events, and academic collaborations played a crucial role in demystifying blockchain technology and its environmental applications. By fostering a culture of transparency and open dialogue, the movement built trust and credibility within the community.

Another important lesson was the need for clear and consistent regulations to support the integration of digital currency and sustainability. The pioneers of the Eco-Coin movement worked closely with policymakers to navigate the complex landscape of international finance and environmental regulations.

Their collaborative approach resulted in the development of guidelines and best practices that facilitated the growth of the Eco-Coin ecosystem. By advocating for regulatory changes that aligned economic incentives with environmental stewardship, the movement ensured its long-term success.

The Eco-Coin movement also highlighted the potential of innovation and technology to drive positive change. The development of the green blockchain, the integration of AI and machine learning, and the creation of decentralized autonomous organizations (DAOs) were just a few examples of the groundbreaking innovations that defined the movement. These technologies offered new opportunities for enhancing the efficiency and effectiveness of sustainable finance, demonstrating the transformative potential of digital currency.

As the Eco-Coin movement continued to evolve, its pioneers remained dedicated to their vision of a more sustainable and inclusive future. They recognized the importance of continuous learning and adaptation, staying ahead of emerging risks and opportunities. By fostering a culture of innovation, collaboration, and transparency, they ensured the long-term success of the Eco-Coin movement and its impact on the global economy.

17

Chapter 17: A Vision for the Future

The story of Eco-Coins and their pioneers is one of vision, innovation, and resilience. It is a testament to what can be achieved when diverse stakeholders come together to address the complex challenges of the 21st century. As the Eco-Coin movement continued to evolve, it remained a symbol of hope and possibility, inspiring future generations to build a more sustainable and inclusive world.

The pioneers of the Eco-Coin movement recognized that their work was far from complete. They continued to push the boundaries of technology, exploring new frontiers in blockchain, AI, and sustainable finance. Their dedication to innovation and collaboration ensured that the Eco-Coin ecosystem remained dynamic and resilient, capable of adapting to new challenges and opportunities.

Looking to the future, the Eco-Coin movement aimed to expand its reach and impact on a global scale. By forging new partnerships and alliances, the pioneers sought to drive sustainable development in diverse contexts and regions. They recognized the importance of fostering a culture of inclusion and empowerment, ensuring that the benefits of Eco-Coins were distributed equitably and that all voices were heard.

The vision for the future of Eco-Coins was one of optimism and determination. The pioneers remained committed to their goal of creating a more sustainable and inclusive global economy. Through their efforts, they demonstrated that it was possible to align economic incentives with environmental stewardship, driving meaningful change on a global scale. The story of Eco-Coins and their pioneers serves as an inspiration for future generations, a reminder that visionary thinking and collaborative action can create a brighter and more sustainable future for all.

"Eco-Coins and Empires: The Billionaires Merging Crypto, Sustainability, and Global Power."

In "Eco-Coins and Empires," you'll journey into a groundbreaking intersection of digital finance and environmental sustainability. This captivating book unveils the stories of visionary billionaires who are transforming our world by merging cryptocurrency with green initiatives. These pioneers are not just chasing profits; they are redefining the future of finance and sustainability through innovative technologies and collaborative efforts.

From the development of the green blockchain to the rise of decentralized autonomous organizations (DAOs), this book explores the technological marvels driving the Eco-Coin revolution. You'll discover how digital currencies designed with sustainability at their core are incentivizing eco-friendly practices and democratizing access to financial systems. Through compelling case studies and global success stories, "Eco-Coins and Empires" highlights the transformative potential of aligning economic incentives with environmental stewardship.

Dive into the intricacies of international collaborations, public-private partnerships, and the role of policy in shaping the future of sustainable finance. The book delves into the challenges and controversies faced by the Eco-Coin movement, offering insights into the resilience and adaptability of its pioneers. With a forward-looking vision, "Eco-Coins and Empires" paints a hopeful picture of a more sustainable and inclusive global economy driven by innovation and collective action.

www.ingramcontent.com/pod-product-compliance
Lightning Source LLC
LaVergne TN
LVHW020457080526
838202LV00057B/6012